AF679906

PMP EXAM MASTERY

30 Cheat Sheets to Pass With Confidence

by **Ryan Richman**

Copyright © 2025 Ryan Richman
All Rights Reserved.

UPDATED FOR PMBOK 7TH EDITION & AGILE GUIDE

PMP

EXAM MASTERY

30 CHEAT SHEETS TO PASS WITH CONFIDENCE

VISUAL GUIDE

AGILE & PREDICTIVE

PMBOK 7 COMPLIANT

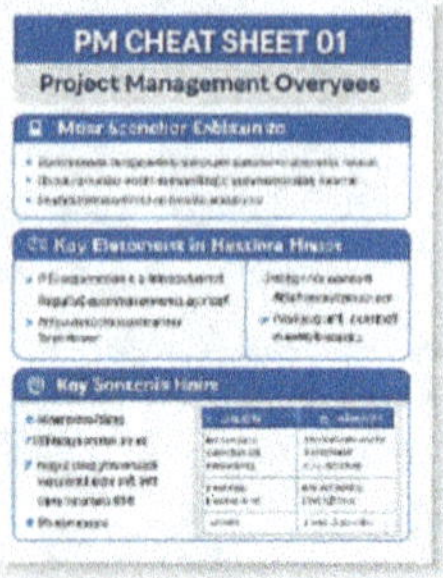

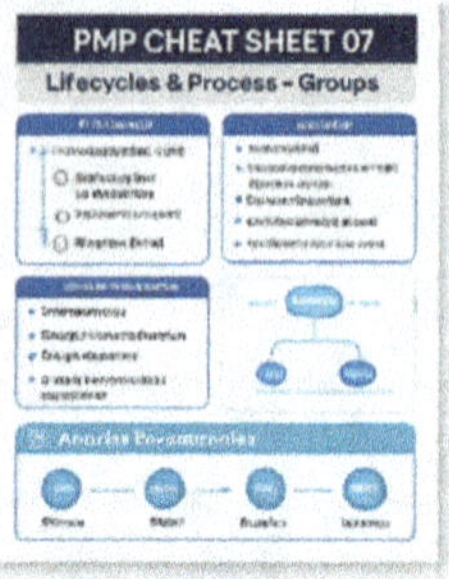

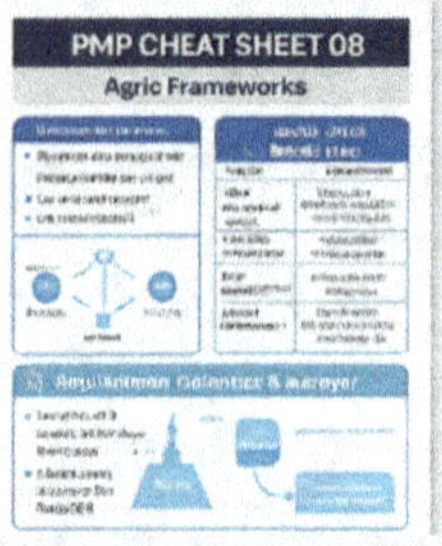

By
Ryan
Richman

INDEX

Why This PMP Manual ______ 5

Why a Complete and Visual PMP Tool ______ 6

How You Can Benefit from This Manual ______ 7

What is PMP and why it's important ______ 11

Why the PMP Is Recognized Worldwide ______ 13

How the PMP Can Transform Your Career ______ 15

Who Should Take the PMP? ______ 16

Why the PMP Certification Matters ______ 17

Structure of the PMP examination ______ 20

Get Ready for the Challenge Ahead ______ 23

Step-by-Step Lessons to Build Real Understanding ___ 25

How Each Lesson Works ______ 26

30 Visual Infographics in Cheat Sheet Style ______ 27

How to Use Them Effectively ______ 28

Final Exam Strategy Tips ______ 31

Master the Visuals ______ 31

BONUS TIPS FOR MEMORY MASTERY ______ 34

What Others Are Saying ______ 35

CHEAT SHEET 01 PMP ______ 37

CHEAT SHEET 02 PMP ______ 38

PMP CHEAT SHEET 03 ______ 39

PMP CHEAT SHEET 04 ______ 40

PMP CHEAT SHEET 05 ______ 41

PMP CHEAT SHEET 06 ______ 42

PMP CHEAT SHEET 07 ________ 43
PMP CHEAT SHEET 08 ________ 44
PMP CHEAT SHEET 09 ________ 45
PMP CHEAT SHEET 10 ________ 46
PMP CHEAT SHEET 11 ________ 47
PMP CHEAT SHEET 12 ________ 48
PMP CHEAT SHEET 13 ________ 49
PMP CHEAT SHEET 14 ________ 50
PMP CHEAT SHEET 15 ________ 51
PMP CHEAT SHEET 16 ________ 52
PMP CHEAT SHEET 17 ________ 53
PMP CHEAT SHEET 18 ________ 54
PMP CHEAT SHEET 19 ________ 55
PMP CHEAT SHEET 20 ________ 56
PMP CHEAT SHEET 21 ________ 57
PMP CHEAT SHEET 22 ________ 58
PMP CHEAT SHEET 23 ________ 59
PMP CHEAT SHEET 24 ________ 60
PMP CHEAT SHEET 25 ________ 61
PMP CHEAT SHEET 26 ________ 62
PMP CHEAT SHEET 27 ________ 63
PMP CHEAT SHEET 28 ________ 64
PMP CHEAT SHEET 29 ________ 65
PMP CHEAT SHEET 30 ________ 66

Why This PMP Manual

Preparing for the PMP exam is one of the most demanding and transformative challenges a professional can undertake. It's not just about earning a certification—it's about proving your ability to lead, deliver value, and adapt in a fast-changing world.

I wrote this manual because I saw too many candidates overwhelmed by hundreds of pages of theory, struggling to connect the dots between concepts and real-life applications. Most resources were either too dense, too abstract, or lacked structure. I wanted to change that.

This manual was created to be clear, visual, and practical. It breaks down complex ideas into manageable lessons and visual cheat sheets so you can learn faster, retain more, and apply the knowledge confidently, whether in the exam or on the job.

My goal is simple:

To give you a complete, concise, and up-to-date guide that helps you pass the exam and grow as a professional.

Whether you're just starting your PMP journey or finalizing your revision, I hope this book becomes your most trusted study companion.

Let's get started—one lesson, one principle, one success at a time.

Why a Complete and Visual PMP Tool

In today's fast-paced world, we don't just need information—we need clarity. I've seen too many project professionals spending hours buried in textbooks, only to realize they're memorizing theory without truly understanding it.

What pushed me to create this tool was a simple idea:

"What if PMP candidates could study smarter—not just harder?"

I wanted to design something that:

- Combines detailed explanations with visual learning
- Helps you see the structure of project management at a glance
- Allows for quick reviews before the exam
- Supports different learning styles, especially for visual and conceptual learners

That's why this manual blends in-depth lessons with high-impact cheat sheets. Each page is crafted to help you:

- Focus on what matters
- Retain key concepts longer
- Develop the mindset of a real-world project leader

Because passing the PMP is not about cramming.

It's about connecting knowledge with purpose, and this book is here to help you do exactly that.

How You Can Benefit from This Manual

This manual was designed to give you a strategic advantage—not just to pass the exam, but to master project management as a discipline.
Here's how you'll benefit:

1. Clear, Step-by-Step Explanations

Each topic is broken down into easy-to-digest lessons, guiding you from the fundamentals to advanced insights. No filler—only what you really need to know, explained with clarity and purpose.

2. Visual Learning Through Cheat Sheets

Every concept is supported by a full-color cheat sheet that summarizes key information visually. These are perfect for:

- Quick review sessions
- Memorization
- Pre-exam refreshers
- Reinforcing connections between ideas

3. Up-to-Date Content Aligned with the Exam

This guide reflects the latest PMP Exam Content Outline, the PMBOK® Guide – 7th Edition, and the Agile Practice Guide. You'll be ready for both predictive and agile/hybrid questions.

4. Built-in Study Strategy

The manual is organized in a progressive learning flow, helping you:

- Understand concepts
- Apply knowledge
- Practice recall
- Review efficiently

5. Exam-Mindset Training

- You'll learn how to:
- Think like a PMP-certified manager
- Tackle situational questions with confidence
- Eliminate wrong choices effectively
- Stay focused and strategic under pressure

6. Career-Ready Knowledge

Beyond the exam, this manual helps you:

- Lead teams more effectively
- Communicate with clarity
- Manage risks and complexity
- Deliver consistent value

Whether you're a first-time candidate or a professional looking to refresh your skills, this book will help you turn preparation into power—and knowledge into results.

A Note to You, the Candidate

If you're reading this, it means you're about to take on a challenge that will transform the way you work, think, and lead.

Preparing for the PMP exam is not easy.

It requires discipline, clarity, and above all, purpose.

This book was written for someone like you:

Someone who wants more than just a title.

Someone who wants to be trusted.

Someone who wants to deliver real value, lead with confidence, and build a career that matters.

You're not alone in this.

I've walked this path. I know the frustration, the overload of material, the moments of doubt.

But I also know the power of preparation, the joy of progress, and the quiet pride that comes when you realize:

"I've got this."

This manual isn't just pages—it's a guide, a companion, and a toolbox.

It was created to make your journey simpler, smarter, and more focused.

Every visual sheet, every lesson, every tip is here to help you cross the finish line—not just with a passing score, but with a transformed mindset.

So take a breath. Turn the page.

Let's build your PMP success story—one chapter at a time.

What is PMP and why it's important

What Is the PMP Certification?

The Project Management Professional (PMP®) is the world's most recognized certification for project managers. Issued by the Project Management Institute (PMI®), it demonstrates that you have the skills, experience, and knowledge to lead projects successfully in any industry, using any methodology.

Why Is It Important?

- Globally respected in over 200 countries
- Recognized across all industries: IT, construction, healthcare, finance, marketing
- Validates your ability to lead teams and deliver results
- Increases your career opportunities and salary potential
- Aligns with both traditional (waterfall) and agile/hybrid approaches

According to PMI, PMP-certified professionals earn up to 32% more than their non-certified peers.

What Does It Represent?

- Mastery of project management concepts, tools, and techniques
- Adaptability in complex and fast-paced environments
- Leadership is based on collaboration, communication, and accountability
- A commitment to continuous improvement and value delivery

Who Should Get the PMP?

- Project Managers
- Team Leads
- Coordinators and Program Managers
- Agile Practitioners

Whether you manage small internal initiatives or large cross-functional programs, the PMP sets you apart as a global professional leader in project delivery.

Why the PMP Is Recognized Worldwide

The PMP® isn't just another certification—it's a global gold standard in project management.
Here's why it holds such authority across industries and countries:

1. Issued by PMI®, a Global Authority

The Project Management Institute (PMI®) is a nonprofit professional organization with members in over 200 countries.
PMI sets the global standards and best practices for project management, and the PMP is its flagship credential.

2. Based on Universal Principles

Unlike certifications limited to specific tools or sectors, the PMP is based on:

- Universal project management principles
- The PMBOK® Guide, which serves as an international framework
- Both predictive and agile/hybrid methodologies

That makes it relevant and applicable across cultures, industries, and borders.

3. ISO Accreditation

The PMP is accredited under ISO 17024, which means it meets international standards for certification of personnel. This adds to its credibility, neutrality, and rigor.

4. Trusted by Leading Organizations

Top global employers—including Google, Amazon, NASA, and the UN—trust PMP as a mark of excellence. It's often a requirement for project leadership roles.

5. Recognized Across Industries

Whether in IT, engineering, finance, healthcare, government, or construction, PMP-certified professionals are in high demand for their ability to:

- Manage complex projects
- Lead diverse teams
- Deliver consistent value

Being PMP-certified signals to employers, clients, and colleagues that you are a qualified, reliable, and globally aligned project leader.

How the PMP Can Transform Your Career

Getting PMP® certified isn't just about adding letters after your name—it's about unlocking your potential as a respected leader in project delivery.

Here's how the PMP can change your professional trajectory:

1. Stand Out in a Competitive Market

In a world full of job titles, the PMP acts as proof of excellence.

It tells employers that you:

- Know how to manage complex projects
- Can lead teams effectively
- Understand both agile and traditional methodologies

You don't just do the job—you lead it.

2. Earn More

According to the PMI Salary Survey:

- PMP-certified professionals earn up to 32% more on average
- The PMP can significantly boost your salary in every region and industry

It's an investment that pays off, year after year.

Bottom line: The PMP is more than a certification. It's a career transformation tool.

It gives you the skills, recognition, and clarity to take your next big step.

Who Should Take the PMP?

The PMP certification is not just for traditional "project managers." It's designed for any professional who leads or contributes to projects, regardless of industry, title, or methodology.

If any of the following describes you, this exam is for you:

Project Managers

You lead projects from start to finish and want formal recognition of your skills.

Team Leaders & Coordinators

You manage people, schedules, or deliverables, even if "project manager" isn't in your job title.

Agile Practitioners

You work in Scrum, Kanban, or hybrid environments and want to demonstrate your versatility.

Business Analysts & Product Owners

You help define scope, gather requirements, and drive stakeholder value.

Consultants & Freelancers

You manage clients, deliver results, and want to stand out in a competitive market.

Professionals Seeking a Career Pivot

You have experience in operations, marketing, tech, healthcare, or engineering, and want to step into a leadership role.

Internal Staff Managing Projects

You've been "accidentally promoted" into project responsibility and need the skills to lead confidently.

If you manage tasks, people, deadlines, and expectations, you're already doing project management.

Getting certified is the next smart move.

Why the PMP Certification Matters

Earning your PMP® is more than passing an exam—it's about elevating your professional identity.

In today's world, where anyone can claim to be a "project manager," the PMP stands out as a formal, globally respected validation of your skills, mindset, and leadership ability.

Here's why it truly matters:

1. It's Recognized Everywhere

The PMP is accepted in over 200 countries and across every industry.

It tells employers and clients:

"This person knows how to lead projects—and deliver results."

2. It Proves You Deliver Value

Project management isn't just task management.

It's about

- Balancing resources
- Managing change
- Creating business impact

The PMP proves you know how to turn strategy into reality.

3. It Signals Mastery, Not Just Experience

Many people have project experience. Few have documented, internationally tested competence.

PMP certification shows you've mastered:

- Predictive (waterfall), Agile, and Hybrid approaches
- Risk, cost, scope, time, communication, and quality management
- Leadership and stakeholder engagement

4. It Opens Doors and Builds Trust

Whether you're applying for a job, leading a team, or managing a high-stakes project, PMP gives you instant credibility.

Colleagues trust your judgment.

Executives listen to your recommendations.

5. It Changes How You Think

The value of PMP is not just technical—it's transformational.

You'll:

- Think strategically
- Make better decisions
- Lead with empathy and clarity
- Navigate complexity with confidence

PMP isn't just a credential—it's a mindset.

It teaches you how to manage not only projects but also uncertainty, people, and pressure.

And that's a skill that transcends industries, borders, and titles.

Structure of the PMP examination

Passing the PMP® exam requires more than knowledge —it requires strategy, time management, and the ability to apply your skills to real-world scenarios. Here's everything you need to know about the format and structure of the PMP exam:

Exam Format Overview

Element Details

Total Questions 180 (instead of the old 200)

Time Limit 230 minutes (3 hours and 50 minutes)

🧷 Breaks Two 10-minute breaks (after Q60 & Q120)

Type of Exam : Computer-based, taken at test centers or online (proctored)

Scoring Score is calculated based on difficulty-weighted questions; no fixed passing score (PMI uses psychometric analysis)

Types of Questions

You'll encounter a variety of question formats, not just multiple choice:

Type Description:

Multiple Choice 1: correct answer out of 4 options

Multiple Response 2–3 correct answers (you must select all correct ones)

Matching (Drag & Drop) Match concepts, terms, or tools

Hotspot: Click on diagrams or images to answer

Fill-in-the-Blank (rare) Complete a sentence with a missing word or number.

Domains and Weighting

The exam is based on the Exam Content Outline (ECO), not just the PMBOK® Guide. It includes three Performance-Domains:

Domain Weight on Exam Focus

People ~42 % Leading, motivating, and managing teams

Process ~50 % Technical project management (scope, risk, etc.)

Business Environment ~8 % Strategy alignment, value delivery, compliance

At least 50% of the questions reflect agile or hybrid approaches.

Key Features to Know

Questions are often situational, asking:

"What should the project manager do next?"

There are no negative marks, so always answer every question

You can flag questions for review and return to them later

Time management is crucial: ~75 seconds per question

Passing Criteria

PMI does not disclose the exact passing score.

Instead, performance is reported as:

Above Target

Target

Below Target

Needs Improvement

Your performance is rated within each domain, not just overall.

Pro Tip:

Don't just study theory. Practice applying concepts to real-life project scenarios. That's what the PMP exam really tests: your ability to think like a project leader.

Get Ready for the Challenge Ahead

Mental Preparation Is Half the Battle

Before you dive into formulas, frameworks, and principles, take a moment to understand the nature of the challenge you're about to face.

The PMP exam is not just a memory test.

It's a test of judgment, mindset, and decision-making under pressure.

What Makes It Challenging?

- It's long: 180 questions over nearly 4 hours
- It's adaptive: No two candidates see the same questions
- It's situational: You're asked to think like a leader, not just a technician
- It's diverse: Questions cover predictive, agile, and hybrid approaches
- It's strategic: You need to manage time, focus, and stress during the test

What You Need to Succeed

To succeed, you'll need more than knowledge. You'll need:

- Clarity on key concepts
- Confidence in your decisions
- Endurance to maintain focus for hours
- Calm under pressure
- Adaptability when a question throws you off balance

Adopt a Success Mindset

- Treat this journey as a professional transformation, not just an exam
- Trust your preparation—and commit to deep understanding, not surface learning
- Replace fear with structure: build a plan and stick to it
- See every practice question as a training opportunity

Remember: The PMP exam rewards those who can think clearly in complexity.

If you're here, reading this, you already have what it takes.

Now it's time to shape your knowledge into action.

-

Step-by-Step Lessons to Build Real Understanding

Not Just What to Learn—But How to Learn It

This manual was designed to guide you through the entire PMP knowledge base with clarity and intention. Each lesson is written to take you step by step from theory to application, giving you the confidence not only to pass the exam but also to apply what you learn in real projects.

What Makes These Lessons Different?

- **Detailed, not overwhelming**

Each topic is broken down into clear, digestible segments, so you'll never feel lost.

- **Structured to reflect how the exam thinks**

You'll learn how PMP concepts connect, not just what they are.

- **Real-world applications**

Situational guidance helps you act like a project leader, not a memorizer.

- **Visual reinforcement**

Every lesson is paired with a cheat sheet that summarizes key ideas at a glance.

How Each Lesson Works

Section What It Does

- **Core Explanation**

teaches you the concept in depth, using examples

- **Step-by-Step Breakdown**

helps you understand how to apply it logically

- **Exam Tips**

Shows how this topic appears on the test

Common Traps

warns you about frequent mistakes and misunderstandings

- **Pro Insight**

offers a real-world interpretation from a PM's perspective

- **Cheat Sheet Link**

Visual recap to aid memory and revision

Whether you're studying with 30 minutes a day or building a 4-week crash plan, these step-by-step lessons will help you stay focused, learn faster, and retain more.

30 Visual Infographics in Cheat Sheet Style

All You Need to Remember—On One Page Each

To help you learn faster and retain more, this manual includes 30 full-color cheat sheets—one for each key PMP topic.

They're not just decorative. They're carefully designed cognitive tools.

What Makes These Cheat Sheets Powerful?

One concept per page

Each sheet focuses on a single core topic, so you can study or review without distraction.

Visual structure for fast memory recall

Charts, diagrams, icons, and color blocks help you see the information, not just read it.

Perfect for last-minute review

Use them the day before the exam or between mock questions to refresh what really matters.

Ideal for visual learners

If you think in images or patterns, these sheets are your secret weapon.

What's Inside Each Infographic?

Element Purpose

Title + Topic Code

Purpose: Helps you locate and organize each subject

Concept Breakdown

Purpose: Short summaries of definitions, tools, and processes

Visual Layout

Purpose: Tables, pyramids, charts, icons for instant clarity

Pro Tips & Warnings

Purpose: Highlight what to focus on—and what to avoid

Optional Diagrams

Purpose: Graphs, timelines, and frameworks for deeper insight

How to Use Them Effectively

- After reading a lesson, review the related cheat sheet
- Print or save your favorites for daily quick reviews
- Use them as memory triggers before mock exams
- Visualize key ideas during the exam—you'll remember the layout isn't a summary. They're accelerators.

At a glance, you'll see what matters most—and remember it when it counts.

How to Think, What to Notice, and When to Trust Your Instincts

Let's be honest—180 questions in 230 minutes is no walk in the park.

But the good news is: the PMP exam follows patterns, and with the right mindset, you can master each section with clarity and control.

Here's how to approach each part of the exam like a pro.

Tips for Tackling Every Section of the PMP Exam

1. People Domain (~42%)

Focus: Leadership, team building, conflict resolution, communication

This section tests your ability to lead—not to boss. Expect questions like:

"A team member is underperforming. What should the project manager do next?"

Tips:

- Always choose collaborative and supportive answers over punitive ones
- Think like a servant leader: your job is to enable the team to succeed
- Prioritize empathy, engagement, and transparency

Many questions are situational: simulate real team dynamics in your head and ask yourself, "What would a calm, competent leader do here?"

2. Process Domain (~50%)

Focus: Scope, schedule, cost, risk, quality, procurement, integration

This is the technical engine of the PMP exam. Expect questions like:

"A change request is submitted during execution. What's the next step?"

Tips:

Know your process flows: what comes before and after each action

Understand the impact of change on cost, time, and quality

Don't memorize—simulate. Think in terms of cause → effect

Review your cheat sheets for the sequencing of actions in each knowledge area

Pro Tip: On these questions, PMI often tests your judgment, not just memory. Think systemically.

Final Exam Strategy Tips

Don't get stuck. Flag tough questions and move on—you'll have time to come back

Use logic. Eliminate 2 obviously wrong choices, then compare the final 2 calmly

Trust your training. Most wrong answers sound "harsh" or "reactive." The right ones are usually proactive, respectful, and grounded in PM principles

Manage your time. Aim for ~1 minute per question. Use the breaks to reset

Remember: The PMP exam is not about being perfect.

It's about demonstrating that you can stay composed, think clearly, and act wisely—even under pressure.

Master the Visuals

A Strategic System to Memorize All 30 PMP Cheat Sheets

Because memory is not just about repetition—it's about structure, variety, and intention.

Memorizing 30 infographics might sound overwhelming at first.

But with the right system, you can turn passive reading into active retention—and actually enjoy the process.

Here's a step-by-step strategy that will help you absorb and retain each sheet's content deeply and efficiently.

PHASE 1:

Understand Before You Memorize (Days 1–10)

"You can't remember what you don't understand."

What to do:

- Read each lesson before reviewing the cheat sheet
- Summarize each concept in your own words (1–2 sentences max)
- Focus on the why behind each visual structure (e.g., pyramid = hierarchy, cycle = process)

Tool: Use a notebook or digital journal titled "My PMP Notes."

Create one page per infographic where you translate the visual into your own logic.

Goal: Create a mental hook for each concept.

PHASE 2: Visual Recall Training (Days 11–18)

"Memory grows through recall, not re-reading."

What to do:

- Pick 5 infographics per day
- Look at each one for 90 seconds
- Then close the book and reconstruct the key points from memory
- Open the page again and check what you missed
- Repeat daily, rotating the groups of 5 to cover all 30 sheets in a 6-day cycle.

Goal: Activate visual memory and long-term retention through "memory retrieval."

PHASE 3: Contextual Practice (Days 19–25)

"Information sticks when it's connected to real action."

What to do:

- After reviewing an infographic, ask yourself:
- "How would this help me solve a situational question on the exam?"
- Create one example scenario for each infographic (can be simple or realistic)
- If possible, verbalize your thinking out loud or explain it to a peer

Goal: Strengthen understanding by applying concepts to simulated real-world use.

PHASE 4: Condensed Flash Review (Days 26–30)

"Speed and repetition create confidence under pressure."

What to do:

- Review 10 sheets per day, but this time:
- Spend no more than 1 minute per sheet
- Say out loud the 3–5 key concepts from memory
- If stuck, check immediately and retry
- By Day 30, your mental map will be sharp, fast, and ready for the exam.

Goal: Achieve rapid recognition and recall under time pressure.

BONUS TIPS FOR MEMORY MASTERY

Use color association: Link each infographic to a color (e.g., green = planning, red = risk)
Create mental images: The more absurd or visual, the more it sticks (e.g., "Stakeholders = orchestra of expectations")
Teach it: If you can explain it clearly to someone else, it's yours forever
Use spaced repetition apps: Tools like Anki or Notion can help automate the review process
Print your top 5 and hang them where you'll see them daily
Remember: You don't need to memorize everything word-for-word.
You need to internalize the logic, see the structure, and recall what's essential—just like a real project manager.

What Others Are Saying

Real Results from Real Professionals

"This manual was a game-changer. I had tried other resources, but nothing helped me visualize and retain the material like these cheat sheets. I passed on my first attempt."

— Elena R., PMP | IT Project Manager, Spain

"I was overwhelmed by the amount of information out there. This book brought clarity. The structure, the visuals, and the step-by-step lessons helped me study smarter, not harder."

— James T., PMP | Construction Planner, Canada

"I work in a hybrid environment with agile teams, and I needed a resource that respected that. This guide didn't just prepare me for the exam—it made me a better project leader."

— Priya K., PMP | Agile Delivery Lead, India

"I had failed the PMP once before. This manual helped me understand what I was missing. The focus on mindset and practical application gave me the confidence I needed."

— Victor M., PMP | Healthcare Project Coordinator, Nigeria

"The visual cheat sheets were a life-saver during revision week. I kept them on my wall and reviewed one each morning. They made a huge difference."
— Lina G., PMP | Marketing Project Lead, UAE

"If you want to pass the PMP without drowning in dry textbooks, this is the manual to get. It's precise, smart, and surprisingly motivating."
— David L., PMP | Business Analyst, USA

These testimonials reflect the voice of learners like you—professionals who turned effort into mastery, and preparation into certification.

PMP CHEAT SHEET 01

Project Management Overview

What is Project Management?

Project Management is the application of knowledge, skills. too ls, and techniques to project activities to meet project requirements. it is achieved through effective management of processes across Svprots-ess groups and ten knowledge areas.

Objectives of Proce Management

- **Deliver value** to stakeholders
- **Ensure project** goals and benfits are met
- **Balance the constraints:**

Time Cost Scope Quality' Resources

Key Concepts to Remember

- **A project** is a **temporary** effort to create a unique product, service, or result
- **Operatives** are ongoing and **repetitive**, unlike projects
- **The PMBOK Guide (7th Edition')** organizes knowledge into **Principles** and **Performance Domains** thathan rigld processes

The 10 Knowledge Areas

Knowledge Area	Description
Integration Mana-gement	Unily and docrdinare all elements
Scope Management	Define what is isn't. included
Schedule Manage-ment	Manage thiwity completion
Cost Management	Contral budget and expenditures
Quality Management	Mest project and stalietion-det espectations
Resource Manage-ment	Manage human and physical
Communication Management	Ensure effective project
Risk Management	communic-attell
Procurement Management	Identity. assess. and respend risks
Stakehoider Management	Acquire and serisly stakeholders

Pro Tip

The PMP exam now emphasizes a hybrid approach-a blend of predictive (waterfall) and adaptive (agile) methods. Be ready to apply the fight approach based on the context.

PMP CHEAT SHEET 02

Project Initiation

Laying the Foundation of a Successfful Project

What is Project Initiation?

Project initiation is the first phase in the project lifecycle.
It defines the project at a high level and authorizes it to begin.
It sets the direction, purpose, and justification for the project

Key Concepts & Terms

Project Selection Methods:

- Benefit-Cost Ratio (BCR)
- Net Present Value (NPV)
- Internal Rate of Retum (IRR)
- Payback Period

Project Charter Contents:

Project purpose and goals
High-level requirements
High-level risks
Assigned Project Manager

Key Concepts & Terms

Document	Purpose
Business Case	Justifies the investment. Why are we doing this project
Benefits Mgint Plan	Describes expected project benefits and how they track
Project Charter	Officially authorizes project
	High-level requirements
High-level requirements	High-level risks
	Stakeholders and roles

Tips to Remember

- The Project Charter formally starts the project.
- The PM is officially authorized to allocate resources oncce the charter is approved
- Key stakeholders must be engaged from the beginning to align expectations

PMP CHEAT SHEET 03

Stakeholder Identification & Analysis

Know Who Matters and How to Engage Them

What Are Stakeholders?

Stakeholders are individuals, groupss, or organizations that can affect or be affected by a project, or perceive themsel ves to be affect(ᴓ), –˜émployeŝ themscles.

Stakeholder Identification

- Performed early in the initiating and refined during Planning.

Tool/Technique

- A living document listing names, roles, influence bow· they'll be tracked

- Project Purpose and ẗuas
- High-level requirements
- Assigned Project Mânáger

Stakeholder Classification

- Power – Authority to Influence the project
- Interst–Level of concern in projed outcomes
- Influencė–Ability to impact deliverables or direction

Pro Tip

Engaging stakeholders early prevents resistance later.

Stakeholder Analysis Dimensions

Knowledge Area	Deacription
Stakeholder Register	A living document
Power/ Interest Grid	Visual tool to classify stakeholders by power
Project Charfer	Gather perceptions *and expectatiors*
Brainstorming & Meetings	Mentify hidden or Indirect stakeholdders
Communication Management	Easeing it will be

Tips to Remember

- The Stakeholder Register is continuously updated throughout the project
- Early identification = better communication =fewer suprises

PMP CHEAT SHEET 04

STAKEHOLDER ENGAGEMENT?

Build Trust, Communicate Often, and Manage Expecttions

WHAT IS STAKEHOLDER ENGAGEMENT?

Stakeholder Engagement is the process of involving stakeholders actively in project decisions and activities throughout the project lifecycle. It includes planning, managing, and monitoring how stakehoiders are involved and kept aligned.

STAKEHOLDER ENGAGEMENT PLAN INCLUDES:

- Stakeholder priorities and influence
- Communication methods and frequency
- Stakeholder roles and responsibllities
- Engagement strategies per stakeholder category
- Escalation and feedback channels

ENGAGEMENT ASSESSMENT MATRIX

Stakeholder	Current Level	Desired Level	Strategy
Sponsor	Supportive	Leading	Involve in decision-making
End Users	Resistant	Supportive	Address concerns communicate
Team Members	Neutral	Engaged	Motivate, clarify contributions

Levels: Unaware / Resistant - Neutral - Supportive - Leading

TOOLS & TECHNIQUES

- Active Listening & Empathy
- Feedback Loops
- Communication Channels
  Emails, dashbeards, status meetings, Workshops

TIPS TO REMEMBER

- Tailor communication style and frequency per stakehcolder
- Engagement is proactive, not reactive

Engagement isn't just about updates — it's about influence and involvement. Focus on building relationships, not just sharing

PMP CHEAT SHEET 05

LEADERSHIP STYLES

DEFINITION

Leadershlp style is a pattern of behavior project leaders use to provide direction, motivate, and effectively influence others.

MANAGEMENT VS. LEADERSHIP

MANAGEMENT	VS.	LEADERSHIP
– Follows procedures		Sets the direction
– Authoritative		Coaching and mentoring
– Focused on stability		Focused on change

LEADERSHIP STYLES

- Laissez-Faire
- Transactional
- Servant Leader
- Transformational
- Charismatic
- Interactional
- Democratic
- Autocratic

LEADERSHIP VALUES

PMP CHEAT SHEET 06

TEAM & WORK ENVIRONMENT

Build High-Performance Teams in Productive Environments

WHAT MAKES A GREAT TEAM?

A project team is a group of individuals with complementary skills workTogether toward a **thommon goal.**

High-performance teams a aligned, motivated, and adaptable.

STAGES OF TEAM DEVELOPMENT (TUCKMAN'S MODEL)

Stage	Team meets, roles unclear
Storming	Conflicts arise, power struggles emerge
Norming	Processes form, cooperation improves
Performing	High trust, productivity and synergy
Adjourning	Project ends, team disbands

KEY ELEMENTS OF EFFECTIVE TEAMS

- Clear Roles and Responsibilities
- Open Communication Channels
- Trust and Psychological Sefety
- Shared Goals and Values
- Supportive Leadership

WORK ENVIRONMENT FACTORS

Physical setup (collocated vs, virtual)

Access to tools and resources

TEAM PERFORMANCE ASSESSMENT TOOLS

- **Team Charter** Defines mission, values, norms, decision-making rules
- **Team Performance Appraisals** Evaluate contributions and collaboration
- **Interpersonal Skills Assessments** Help understand team dynamics

TIPS TO REMEMBER

- A strong **team culture leads to** fewer conflicts and better outcomes.
- Encourage **diversity of thought** and celebrate wins together.

PMP CHEAT SHEET 07

Leadership Styles

What Is Leadership Style?

A leadership style is a rattern of behaviolor a pioject leaoeleader uses to provide direction, motivate team members, and influence project outcomes.

Management vs. Leadership

- Fands-off approarch
- Focused on change and inspiration
- Empathic and peopple-centered

Core Values of Effective leaders

- Vision
- Integrity
- Accountability
- Empathy
- Adaptability
- Innovation

Pro Tip

The most successful leaders blend multiple styles to sult team dynamics and project challenges.

Common Leadersh Styles

Style	Description
Laissez-Faire	Hands-off approach
Transactional	Based on structured tasks and reward/
Transformational	Based as stronge talics and. reward/puntistion
Servant Leader	Focuses on team endees its directtive
Charismatic	Endures decisions inde-penodent
Democratic	Involves team in oc- cisions, encourages
Autocratic	Adapts lacitm or dereguative aproct
Situational	Adapts leadernip.con mutuar/cnt

Tips to Remember

- No single style fits all projects. Adapt based on the situation and team.
- Empowering the toam fosters trust and high performance.

PMP CHEAT SHEET 08

Power Types

What is Power in Project Management?

Power is the ability to influence the behavior of others or the course of events. Project Managers use different types of pw-wer depending on the context, team, and organizational culture.

Types of Power

Power Type	Description
Legitimate	Based on position or formal authority
Reward	Based on ability to provide incentives or benefits
Coercive	Based on ability to penalize or apply negative consequences
Expert	Based on knowledge, skills, or expertise
Referent	Based on charisma, admiration, or respect from others
Informational	Based on control or access to valuable information

Tips to Remember

- Relying solely on legitimate or coercive power may redu'e trust
- Expert and referent power are most effective for long-term influence
- Adjust your power style based on the team's maturity and

Tips to Remember

Relying solely on leqitimate or coercive power may reduce trust

- Expert and referent power are most effective for long-term influence
- Adjust your power style based on the team's maturity and expectations

PMP CHEAT SHEET 09

TEAMWORK & COLLABORATION

What is Teamwork in Projects

Power refers to the cooperative effort of agroup, to echieve a common goal, In project managemenı msents the smoot integration of skills, knowledge and responsibilitiees.

Benefits of Effective Collaboration

- Improved decision-making...
- Faster problem-solving
- Enhanced creativity anJ inova
- Stronger comn'itment
- Faster problem-solving
- Higher team morale

Core Principles of Collaboration

Mutual Respect – Acknowledge everyon's input
Open Communication – Foster transparency and elarity
Shared Accountability – Collective ownership of outcomes
Trust Building – Be reliable, consistent, and
Constructive Feedback – Improve without blame

Tools to Support Collaboration

Tool Type	Examples
Communication	Slack, Microsoft Teams, Zoom, Emaii
File Sharing	Google Drive. SharePoint. Dropbox
Project Tracking	Jira, Trellc. Asana. Manday.com
Knowledge Sharing	Wikis, Notion, Confluence

Tips to Remember

Celebrate team wins to reinforce unity – Promotie actifigences
Handle conflicts promptly and respectfully
Clarify roles to avoid overlap and confusion

PMP CHEAT SHEET 10

Team Motivation

What Is Team Motivation?

Team motivation is refers to the internal an external factors that stimulate team members to be committed to the project's goals and give their best per formance.

Motivational Theories in Project Management

Maslow's Hierarchy
Motivation based on ofulllling f ne levels of needs

Herzberg's Two-Factor
Motivation = preserise oe of sattifiers; demotivation = absence

McGregor's Theory X/Y
Theory X: People dislike vork[illegible]ework
Theory Y: People are self-motivatad

McClelland's Theory
Motivation driven by Nefor Achievement, Afriliation, or Power.

How to Motivate Your Team

Set clear, meaningful goals
Recognize and reward achievements

Encourage autonomy and ownership

Provide feedback and coaching

Foster a supportive team environment

Align tasks with individual strengths

Tips to Remember

- Motivation is not one-size-fits-fill– personnalized
- Avoid micromanagemenc- it reduces trust
- Public recognition boosts mora-ale

Tips to Remember

- Motivation is not one-size-fits-all, personalize it
- Public recognition boosts morale
- Motivated teams take initiative and stay focused

PMP CHEAT SHEET 11

Development Approaches

What Are Development Approaches?

Development approaches ddefine how prroject work is plan and and executed. The choice of approach depends on factors like project complexity, uncertaifny, stkehder lder involvement, and delivery expectations.

Three Main Types of Development Approaches

Approach	Description	Best Used When...
Predictive (Waterfall)	Work is defined up-front, sequential phases	Requirements are stable and well-defined
Iterative	Cycles of build and feedback before final pd	Requirements evolve with feedback
Incremental	Reliverables released with feedback	Early value delivery is important
Agile	Adaptive, flexible, high stakeholder collaboration	Parts of the project differ in complexity
Hybrid	Combines predictive + agile or others	Parts of the project differ in complexic

Key Criteria for Selecting an Approach

- Stakeholder involvement
- Clarity and stability of requirements
- Speed to rqiversanice
- Need for flexibility or cotrol

Tips to Remember

Don't force Agile whereiL.lit doesn't fit. The right approach improves outcomes, reduces waste, and aligns expectations.

PMP CHEAT SHEET 12

Lifecycles & Proces Groups

What Is a Project Lifecycle?

The series of phases a project goes through from itiniation s to closure. It provides a structured approach to deliviring

Common Lifecycle Models

Liffecycle Type	Description
Predictive	Phases are sequential and ire-definedized
Iterative	Repeated cycles to réfinine deliverables
Inoremental	Delivers in parts with stakeholder collaborat onal and feedback
Agile	Short iterations cwith stakeholder collabor ation and feedback
Hy brid	Combines two or or more llfecycle models

Lifecycle vs. Process Groups

- Use lifecycle models to manage complexity and change
- Process groups help ensure 'consistency and control
- Always align lifecycle choice with project context

Think of the lifecycle as the roadmap and the **process groups** as the engine

The 5 Process Groups

Infitating	Define and approite
Planning	Establishes scope. fa-biriets, and procedures
Executing	Complete the project work as planned
Monitoring & Controlling	Track. re-view, and/l tegulate progress
Closing	Finalizes all activities and formally close the

Pro Tip

Think of the lifecycle as the **roadmap** and the process groups

PMP CHEAT SHEET 13

Agile Frameworks

What Is Agile?

A amindset and approach that focuses on customer collaboration, adaptability, and incremental delivery. It's ideal for projects vet evolving requirements and high stakeholder involvement.

Popular Agile Frameworks

- Individuals and interactions over processes and tools
- Working software over comprehensive documetation
- Collaborate with hange over following a plan

Scrum Roles & Events (Overview)

• **Roles:**	Product Owner Scrum Master Development Team
• **Events**:	Sprint, Sprint Planning Daily Scrum, Sprint Review
• **Artifacts:**	Product Backlog Sprint Backlog increment

Three Main Types

Errework	Description from the *Agle.)*
Scrum	Product Owner
Kanban	Scrum Master Development
XP (Extreme Programml)	Sprint Sprint Plannin Daily Scrum Sprint Review.
SAFe	Product Backlog
LeSS	Sprint Backlog Increment

Tips to Remember

- Agile is not just a method -it's culture of flexibility and feedback
- Stakeholders must be actively involved throughout thetrolect
- Agile works best wh en teams are empowered and self-organizing

Pro Tip

PMP CHEAT SHEET 14

Scrum

What Is Scrum?

Scrum is a lightweight and approvce that helps'tcsus revlace itertivetly and incremenent dilerabbility. It's ideal for coliabortion, transparency, and continuous improvement.

Scrum Roles

Product Owner
Defines the proout backlog, prioritizes needs

Scrum Master
Facilltates Scrum pocess, removes impediments

Development Team
Cross-functional, self-organizing team deliverencts

Scrum Events

Role	A time-boxed development cycle (1-4 weeks)
Purpose	Define what will be delivered and how
Daily Scrum	15-minute meeting to inspect progress and adapt
Sprint Review	Presents increment to stakeholders gether feedback

Scrum Artifacts

- **Product Backlog**
  Ordered list of all desrired features
- **Sprint Backlog**
  Iterns selected for current spint
- **Increment**
  Completed work meeting the Definition of Done

✓ Tips to Remember

Scrum thraives in environments of" trust, collaboration, and continuous delivery.

Pro Tip

PMP CHEAT SHEET 15

Requirements Collection & Analysis

What Are Requirements?

Requirements are documented needs and expectations of stakeholders that the project must fulfil.
They guide the project scope and success creriteia.

Types of Requirements

Category	Description
Business Requirements	High-level needs of the organization
Stakeholder Requirements	Needs of individual or groups involv
Solution Requirements	Features for rutu/le- to future state
Transition Requirements	Transition rechange asenc important
Project Requirements	Completed value ising implicant

Techniques for Requirements Collection

Techniques for Requirements Collection
Interviews
Workshops
Focus groups
Surveys & Questionnaires
Observation (Job Shadowing)
Document Analysis
Mind Mapping
Brainstorming

Best Practices

- Engage stakeholders early and frequenity
- Use visuals (models, diagrams) to clarify complex needs
- Prioritize requirements using MoSCoW or Value-Risk Matrix
- Validate and document all assumptions

Pro Tip

Requirements are the foundation of scope. Get them right, and you reduce rework, delays, and dissatisfaction.

PMP CHEAT SHEET 16

Schedule Development (Predictive)

What Is Schedule Development?

Schedule development invoives defining, sequencing and estimating activities, und creating a realistic projectineline under the predictive (waterfall) approach.

Key Tools & Techniques

Tool/Techniquee	Purpose
Work Breakdown Structure (WBS)	Breaks projecto mariage conponets
Activity List	Lists all project tasks devilerables
Network Diagrams	Creates on adivitty and depends
Critical Path Method (CPM)	identifY longestpiṭh of attcivites
Gantt Charts	Float showing activity timing
Leads & Lags	Adjust activity timing
Float (Slack)	Use mietstones tomacounts

Common Estimation Techniques

Analogous Estimating – Base onsitmral βacks or cMead
Parametric Estimating – Uses milestones to mark key
Three-Point Estimating (PERT) events

Tips to Remember

- Define clear activity dependencies (FS, SS, FF, SF)
- Critical Path = zero float
- Update schedule regularl; with actual data
- Use milestones to mark key events

PMP CHEAT SHEET 17

Schedule Development (Adaptive)

What Is Adaptive Scheduling?

In adaptive (Agile) environments, scheduling is-flexible arl iterative. Ut promotes a realistict prioject-times (under tet-mination or sprínts), und liem to deliver value con-u-tuuously and deliver value continuont.

Core Concepts

Concept	Description
Timeboxing	Fixed duration period (e.g.)
Rolling Wave Planning	Long-term wo broadly
Backlog Refinement	Prioializatant and clarificd
Velocity	Bun-throingt rementing
Burn-down Chart	Tracks requirements

Sprint Scheduling Flow

1. **Product Backlog**
   Fixed-duration periods (e.g. 2-weeks)
2. **Sprint Planning**
   Select and commrndo
3. **Sprint Execution**
   Encluscint and crivork
4. **Velocity**
   Burn-down chart
5. **Daily Stand-Ups**
6. **Sprint Retrospective**

Tips to Remember

- Adaptive scheduling embraces change and feedback
- Each sprint delivers working product
- Focus on prioritization, communication, and transparency

Pro Tip Plan just enough to start, then adapt frequen-tly. The goal is to deliver what the customer

PMP CHEAT SHEET 18

Estimation Techniques

What Is Estimation?

Estimation is the process of predicting time, cost, resources, or effort required to complete project activities.

Accurate estimation supports realistic planning and execution.

Common Estimation Techniques

Technique	Description
Analogous Estimating	Based on historial data from sal
Parametric Estimating	Uses statistical relatioftios. e.g. cos, poss-imits)
Three-Point Estimating (cos time/l alues)	Forulvas $E = \frac{O + 4M + P}{6}$
Bottom-Up Estimating	Continual consenssum our experts
Expert Judgment	Based expertience mong a panel
Delphi Technique	Insvolff impncvertuntly

Tips for Choosing the Right Method

- Use Analogous when data is limited.
- Use Parametric when reepatable unfexist
- Use Bottom-Up for accuracy (but it's time tensive)
- Use Delphi or Expert Judgment for uncertain or new domains

Best Practices

- Document assumptions and constraints
- Combine methods for cross-validation
- Involve experienced team members
- Re-estimate periodically as the project evolves

PMP CHEAT SHEET 19

Prioritization Techniques

Why Prioritize?

Prioritization helps teams decáde, what to do first" when time, budget, or resources are limited. It ensures value delivery, clarit, y, and alignment with stakeholder needs.

Popular Prioritization Techniques

Technique	Description
MoSCoW	Clessifies requirements into: Must hofve Should have, Could have
Kano Model	Categorizes features baseed on customer satisfaction
Value-Risk Matrix	Plots items by their value and risk to jrioritize critical work
Weighted Scoring	Assigns numeric scores based on factors (cost, value, effort
100-Point Method	Stakeholders distribute 100 points among options
Elsenhower Matrix	Urgent vs. Important: Hol prioritize time-sensitive work

Tips to Remember

- Involve stakeholders in prioritization process
- Re-evaluate priorities regor-gerly
- Use visual tools to aalign the team

Tips to Remember

- Document stakeholdary regularly
- Use visual tools to align the team
- Combine qualitative (discuss]-on)and quant/tative (scoring)

PMP CHEAT SHEET 20

Monitoring Work

What Is Monitoring in Project Management?

Involves tracking, reviewing, and reporting project performance to ensure that the project stays allgned with the plan and goals it enables early detection or issues.
and facilitates informed decision-maiiking.

What Should You Monitor

- Measure actual performance vs, plann
- Identify deviations and risks early
- Ensure accountubility and progress
- Facilitate communication with stakehol
- Support forecasting and replanning

What Should You Monitor?

Scope

Planneds vs. actual dates, milestones

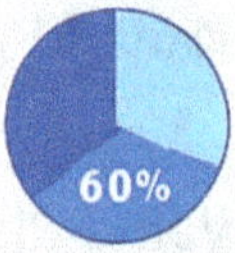

What Should You Monitor?

Scope	Schedule	Cost	Quality
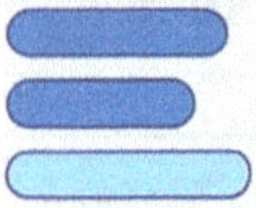	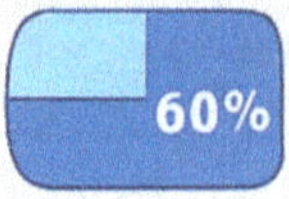		
Planned vs. actual dates milestones	Planned vs. actual expend-iture	Defects, rework, test results	Resource usage, availlability, workload

Best Practices

- Set KPIs and thresholds
- Use dashboards for visibility
- Autornate data collection when possible
- Use dashboards for visibility
- Automate data collection when possible
- Involve team in interpreting trende

PMP CHEAT SHEET 21

Managing Knowledge

What Is Knowledge Management?

Knowledge Management involves creation, sharing, and use of knowledge to support project outcomes. It include brboth expiicit knowledge (documents, data) and tacit knowledge (experience,insigs)

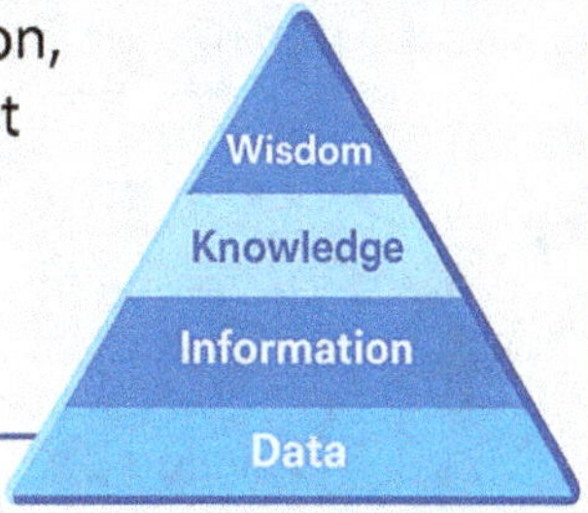

Knowledge Pyramid

Types of Knowledge

Type	Description
Explicit	Easy to documennt, codify, and share
Tacit	Personal, experience-based, harder to express

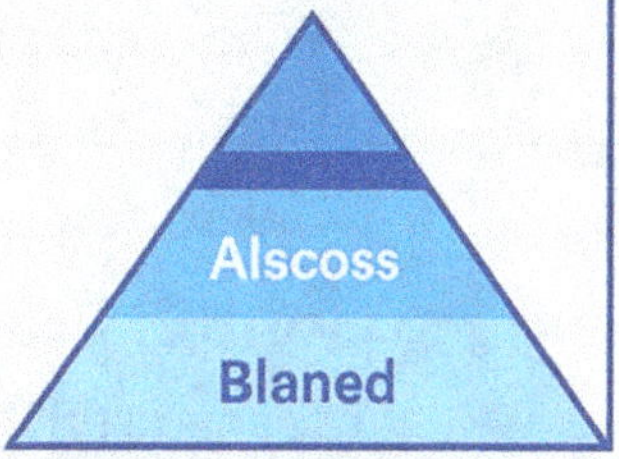

Knowledge Management Activities

- **Knowledge Creation**
  Brainstorming, innovation experimentation
- **Knowledge Sharing**
  Meetings, communities of practice, tools
- **Knowledge Appliication**
  Using insights to guide project decisions
- **Knowledge Storage**
  Document repositonsies, wikis, databases

Tips to Remember

- Encourage a culture of openness and curiosity
- Capture key insights before team disbands
- Balance ″formal systems with informal knowledge

Pro Tip

Your team already holds valuable insights –capture them before they walk out the door.

PMP CHEAT SHEET 22

Conducting Procurements

5 What Is Procurement in Projects?

Procurement involves tracciing, ad required goods s services from outside the organization to ensure that project stay aligned with r pan–under closing vendor contracts.

1 Procurement Process Overview

1 Define what needs to be procured
2 Decide contract types
3 Develop procurement documents

2 Conduct Procurement

1 Solicit bida or proposals
2 Evaluate and select vendòrs
3 Award contracts

3 Control Procurement

1 Manage relationships and contract performance, performance
2 Monitor deliverables
3 Handle changes and disputes

4 Close Procurement

1 Confirm fulfillment
2 Resolve open items
3 Final payments and documentation

Key Procurement Documents

Document	Purpose
Request for Proposal (RFP)	Ask for vendor solutions à pricing
Request for Quotation (RFQ)	Ask for pricing on known spees
Statement of Work (SOW)	Detalls what the salar must deliver
Procurement Management Plan	Defines strategy, ralier and timing

Vendor Evaluation Criteria

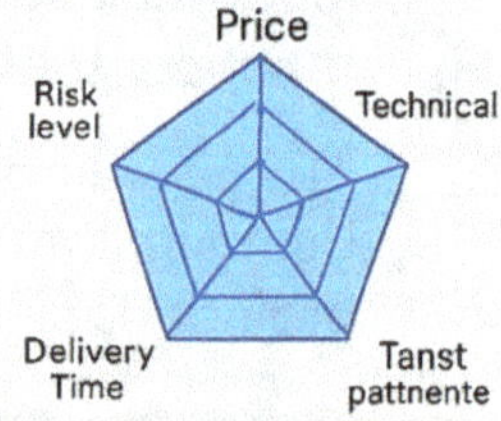

Tips to Remember

Use the right contract for the situation
Evaluate vendors fairly and transparently

Pro Tip Good procurement is not just about price—it's about value, reliability, and risk management.

PMP CHEAT SHEET 23

Contract Types

Why Contract Type Matters

The type of contract defines tost x. risk -risk, & resources distribution between buyer and seller. Choosing the right oh helps manage budget, performance, and uncertainity.

Main Types of Contracts

Fixed Price (FP)	**Cost Reimbursable (CR)**
Set price for an elteretire work	Seller reimbursed for costs + fee
• Firm Fixed Price (FFP) Price is not subject to change	• Buyer bear mdst risk
• Fixed Price Incentive Fee (FPIF) Bonus for achieving performance targets	• Cost Plus Fixed Fee (CPIF) Fixed fée + actual costs Low seller incentive • Shared risk
• Cost Plus Incentive Fee (CPIF) Bonus for cost savings or performance • Shared risk	• Cost Plus Award Fee (CPAF) Subjective award based on buyer evauiation Buyer discretion
Time & Material/s (TM)	Shared/varible
Hourly or daily rate + materials	
• Shared/varyablie risk	

Tips to Remember

✓ Fixed Price shoulda scope is clear add cfinined
✓ T-M is Rimbursable for innovation or research projects
✓ T&M is flexible but keep monitor

Pro Tip

Always matcontract type to project and clarity.

PMP CHEAT SHEET 24

Project Delivery

What Is Project Delivery?

Project delivery refers to the method used to, **plan, execute.** and **transfer the final deliverable** to the client or end user. It ensures the expected value is achieved on time, within scope, and budget.

Key Elements of Project Delivery

Method	Description	Use Case
Waterfall (Predictive)	Sequential, phase-based delivery	Stable, well-defined projects
Agile (Iterative/ Incremental)	Value delivered in short cycles with continuous feedback	Rapid change, evolving requirements
Hybrid	Combines predictive and adaptive methods	Projects with mixed complexity
Design-Build	Single contractor for design & execution	Fast-traek construction or technical work
Public-Private Partnership (PPP)	Shared risk & reward between public and prseter	Government-funded infrastructure

Tips to Remember

- Define **delivery criteria** early
- Use **checklists** for handover **completteness**
- Ensure **support** and **training plans** are imlace

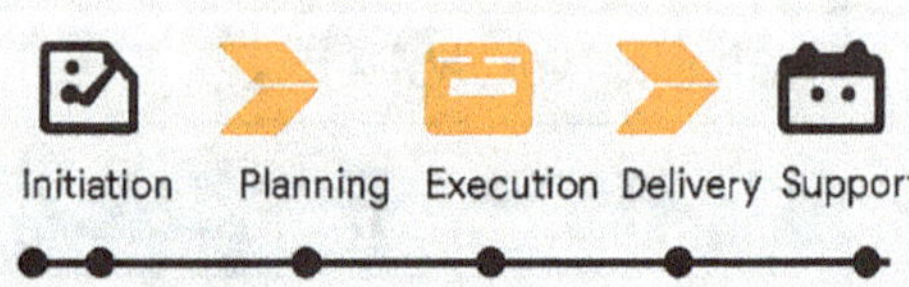

Pro Tip

Delivery is not just about handing over a product—it's about transferring **value** with confidence.

PMP CHEAT SHEET 25

Meeting Quality Requirements

What Is Quality in Project Management?

Quality is the clegree to a project's deliverables meet requirements and expectations. It's

not about perfection–It's about fitnes s *for* use or customer satisfaction.

Key Quality Con cepts

Concept	Description
Cost of Quality (CoQ)	Total cost oof conformance and
Quality Assuran-ce (QA)	Ensures processes are followed
Quality Control (QC)	Inspects delliere-ables to identify
Continuous Improvement	Uses methods like PDCA, Lean, Six ꞉n
Prevention over Inspection	Designing quality in, thathan fixing later

Quality Tools & Technues

- Flowcharts
- Pareto Diagrams
- Control Charts
- Check Sheets
- Fishbone Diagrams (Issikaiaw)
- Scatter Diagrams

Cost of Quality Breakdown (Suggested: Pie Chart)

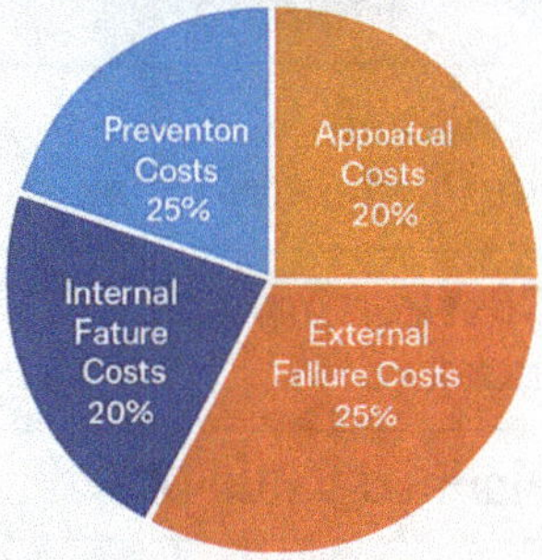

- Prevention Costs **25%**
- Appraisal Costs **20%**
- Internal Failure **30%**
- External Failure Costs **25%**
- Scatter Diagrams

Tips to Remember

Involve shtakedcors ar defining quality criteria

Set measurable quality metrics early

PMP CHEAT SHEET 26

Performance Measurement

Track, Evaluate, and Adjust for Project Success

? What Is Performance Measurement?

Performance measurement is the process of evaluating project progress using quantifiable indicators to ensure objectives are being met and to support decision-making.

Key Performance Indicators (KPIs)

Indicator	What It Measures
Schedule Performannce Index	Efficiency of time used (SPI = EV / PV)
Cost Performance Index (CPI)	Cost efficiency CPI = EV / AC
Planned Value (PV)	Value of work planned to be done
Earned Value (EV)	Value of work actually completed
Actual Cost (AC)	Cost actually incurred

How to Interpret SPI & CPI

Index Value	Interpretation
>1	Ahead of schedule/ under budget
=1	
<1	On schedule/ on budget ”
<1	

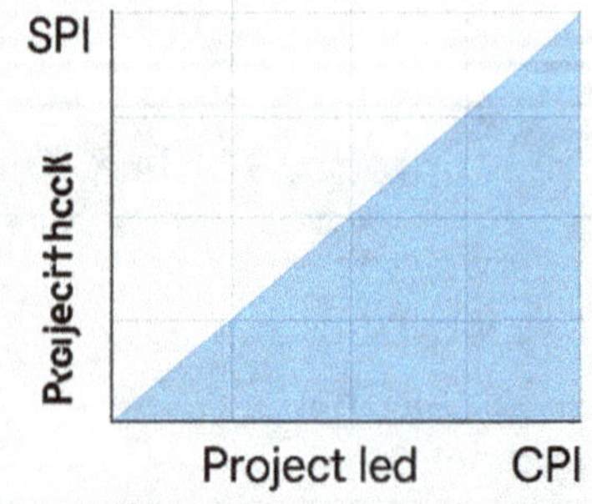

Pro Tip Numbers alone aren't enough. *Interpret trends* and link KPIs to actions and forecasts.

PMP CHEAT SHEET 27

Metrics & KPIs

Measure What Matters Most

What Are Metrics & KPIs?

Metrics are standard units of measurement. Key Performance Indicators (KPIs) are the most relevant metrics that help track progress, performance, and alignment with goals.

Characteristics of Good KPIs

- Relevant – Aligned with project goals
- Measurable – Quatifiable and trackable
- Actionable – Linked to specific responses
- Time-bound – Includes deadlines or time-frammes
- Visible – Easily communicatt'ed to stakeholders

Categories of Project KPIs

Category	Example KPI
Schedule	On-time task completion %
Cost	Cost variance, cost pet. index
Scope	% of scope delivered vs. basel
Quality	Defect density, test pass rate
Team	Resource utilization, engagement
Risk	Number of issues open vs. resolved

Tips to Remember

- Don't measure everything – focus on critical success factors
- KPIs should support predictive and corrective actions

Pro Tip

If a metric isn't driving action or decision-making, it's just "data noise". Make your metrics meaningful.

PMP CHEAT SHEET 28

UNCERTAINTY & RISK

What Is Uncertainty in Projects?

Uncertainty is the lakcof knowledge about future eventsor conditions It is the foundaton of project risk It's indot aut prrnelahely or tangatively affect project objectives.

Types of Risk

Type	Description
Threats	Negative risks that may hinder objectives
Opportunities	Positive risks that may enhance project success
Known Unknowns	Identified risks with unknown timing or impact
Unknown Unknowns	Completely unforeseen events (e.g. black swans)

Visual *Suggestion:* Risk Heat Map

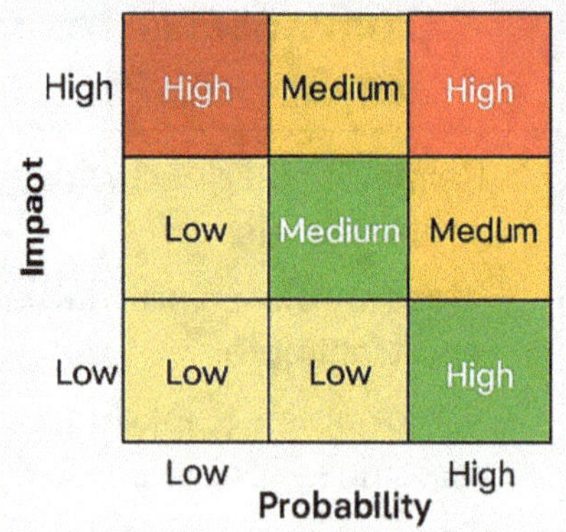

Managing Uncertainty

- Use progressive elaboration to refine understanding
- Conduct risk workshops and brainstorming
- Maintain a risk register
- Perform quantitative and qualitative analysis

Tips to Remember

- Not all risks are bad — exploit opportunities
- Update risk data regularly
- Prioritize based on impact and likelihood

Pro Tip

Risk management is not a one-time task. It's a continuous discipline. Identify early, act quickly, and adjust as you gc.

PMP CHEAT SHEET 29

Risk Management

⚠ What Is Risk Management?

Risk management is systernatic process of identifying, analyzing, planning, and monitoring risks throughout the project.
It helps increase the likellhood of positive events and recduce negative impacts

Risk Management Process

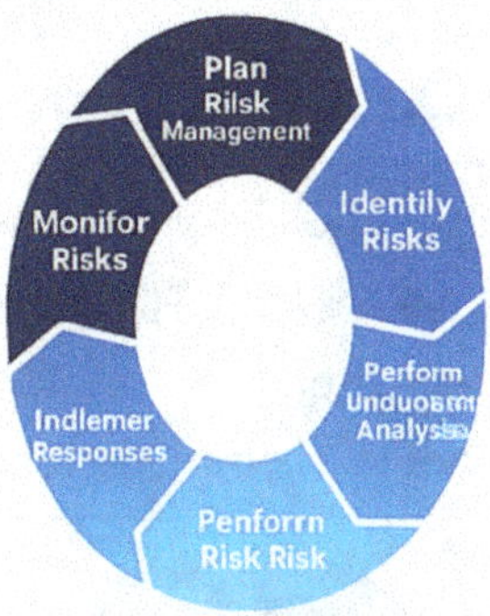

Step	Description
Plan Risk	Hoæ to approach risks in terview'a impact
Perform Qualita-tive Analysis	Rrao threstsinin.chekistss SWOT, Escalate
	Exploit, Enhance, Share Accept, Escalate

Risk Response Strategies

Threats:	Avold, Mitigate, Transfer, Aocept, Escalate
Opportunities:	Exploit, Enhance, Share, Accept, Escalate

Tips to Remember

- Include positive risks (opportunitties) in your v. planning
- Create a risk register and keep it updated
- Tallor responses based on impact, cost. and urgency

Pro Tip Great projects don't avoid risk—they manage it proactively. Planning ahead gives you the power to ad react.

PMP CHEAT SHEET 30

Exam Tips & Tricks

Before the Exam

- ✓ Un derstand the Exam Domains: People, Process, and AgilePract-ice Guide-for quick revision
- ✓ Review the PMBOK® Guide–7th Edition a Agile Practice Guide
- ✓ Practice with mock exams/mind maps for quick revision
- ✓ Use cheat sheets and mind maps for quick .
- ✓ Memorize key formulas procss flows
- ✓ Focus on Agile, Hybrid , and Situatiomal questions

During the Exam

Strategy	Benefit
Time Managent	Benefit feacoust fr timer
Mark and Move	Elfimit d'hickes Narrow down
Eliminatior Choices	Eceroro in"awey." only, etc.
Read Carefully	Read carefuly bie keywords feel

Question Types

- Multiple choice (single answer)
- Multiple-response (2–3 correct)
- Drag-an-drop
- Hotspot (clickon image/diagram)

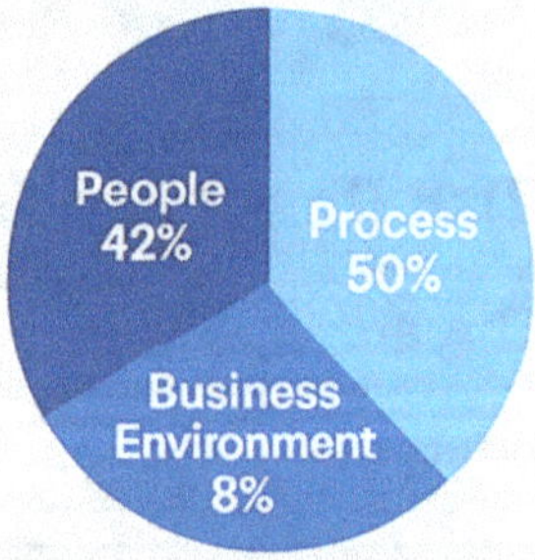

Mindset Tips

- Think like a servant leader, noth a boss
- Prioritize value delivery and team collaboration

- Tuthink like a servant leader, ńŏt a aboss
- Prioritize value delivery and team collaboration

Pro Tip The PMP exam doesn't just test memory—it tests judgment. Focus on what the best project manager do